style to go Bed & Bath

style to go

Bed & Bath

JOSH GARSKOF

The Taunton Press

The Taunton Press
Inspiration for hands-on living®

The Taunton Press, Inc., 63 South Main Street,
PO Box 5506, Newtown, CT 06470-5506
e-mail: tp@taunton.com

Jacket/Cover design: Allison Wilkes
Interior design: Kimberly Adis, Allison Wilkes
Layout: Cathy Cassidy

Library of Congress Cataloging-in-Publication Data
Garskof, Josh.
  Style to go-- bed & bath / Josh Garskof.
     p. cm.
  ISBN-13: 978-1-56158-935-7
  ISBN-10: 1-56158-935-7
  1. Bedrooms. 2. Bathrooms. 3. Interior decoration. I.
Title. II. Title: Style to go. III. Title: Bed & bath. IV. Title:
Style to go-- bed and bath.

NK2117.B4G37 2007
747.7'7--dc22

                                              2006020157

Printed in China
10 9 8 7 6 5 4 3 2 1

contents

style
in the
bedroom

A bed skirt hides the box spring—and everything you've got stashed under the bed.

Water-themed motifs (left) and natural materials such as a bamboo bed and sisal rug (below) are two very different ways to create a beach aesthetic for a home near the water.

All mattresses
need to be turned
in order to
even out the wear—
even "no-flip" products
should be rotated
from head to foot every
6 months or so.

A master bedroom sitting area allows you to spend relaxing moments in your private space even when you're not readying for bed or getting dressed.

Above Sunny orange and yellow walls brighten an attic bedroom that has only one small window.

Right Rich wall colors make a white bed and light-colored fabrics "pop"— which is just what white backdrops do for bold-colored objects.

Above Reds and purples create an invigorating atmosphere—and they're flattering to most skin tones.

Left Simple maple furniture, neutral colors, and wide sliding glass doors all help to enlarge an undersized bedroom.

Above A shallow cubby cut into the wall above a headboard creates a space-saving alternative to a night table.

Right Setting a bed into an alcove behind drapery panels gives a little girl more than a place to rest—it's her own private hideaway.

Above An irresistible choice for little girls' rooms, pink looks best when presented in varying hues and with a strong accent color like green.

Left Limiting the palette to a trio of colors prevents lively hues from overwhelming each other. Here, orange serves as the primary color, lime green as a secondary color, and lemon yellow as an accent.

Silver details, such as the upholstery tacks on the headboard, pick up the metallic hue of the curtain rod while its glass ball finials play off of the table lamps.

A private balcony in a bedroom
is the latest must-have feature,
but you can create a similar look
with floor-to-ceiling windows.

Babies have an emotional response to color, and orange creates feelings of warmth and contentment.

Purple isn't only for kids' rooms. Here, a soft hue and sophisticated wallpaper pattern create a totally adult décor.

Hand-painted wall stripes and floor squares offer two different textures that embellish a purple-and-white color scheme.

A pair of bold hues—red as the primary color and blue as the secondary color—repeat throughout this bedroom.

Whites, beiges,
tans, light browns,
and natural stones and woods
are essential
decorating tools
because they can
harmonize with all other colors.

A faux bois
(French for false wood)
fabric print anchors this
bedroom's décor.

Neutral walls and
linens help to highlight
the intricate carvings
of a dark wood
canopy bed.

Choosing a sophisticated pink instead of the pastel version typical for babies' rooms will give this paint job staying power as the child gets older.

Opposite A high-contrast mix of geometric patterns—curves, zigzags, polka dots,and checks—yields an engaging theme.

Top left The carved floral motifs of these headboards inspired the print used for the bedspreads and drapes.

Bottom left Striped wallpaper plays off the fence-like design of the headboards, tying together the elements of the room.

Soothing blue-and-white color schemes create serene bedroom atmospheres.

Opposite Pale yellow remains quietly in the background, allowing the furnishings to take center stage.

Left Green is not generally considered a neutral color, but it goes with anything. After all, in nature, green foliage combines with countless flower colors.

Color creates mood—
from formal to casual,
energetic to peaceful.

Eye-popping colors give this child's room one-of-a-kind personality.

A multi-hued carpet can establish a color palette for your bedroom. Pick up its colors for the walls, bedding, and other elements.

A colorful border of paint or wallpaper around the top of a child's bedroom dresses up walls without over-saturating the décor.

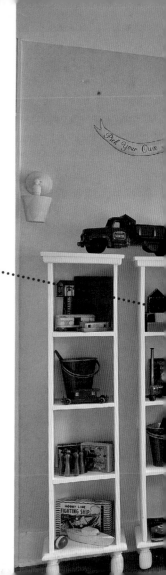

Cheerful checks, stripes, and polka-dots turn a hand-me-down dresser into the focal point of a boy's bedroom.

For a crib tucked under the eaves of an attic bedroom, a painted mural takes the place of a mobile because it's close enough for the youngster to see.

Left Neutral yellow walls harmonize with a nursery-rhyme themed baby's room—as they will with future decorations as the child matures.

Solid-colored bedding was mandatory for the ornate scrollwork on this metal bed, but monogrammed shams and a neighboring oriental rug pick up the theme.

furnishing the bedroom

In compact bedrooms, simple round tables make multifunctional alternatives to standard nightstands.

The top of a
nightstand should be
within 2 in. of the
mattress height,

so it's easy

to set down a book

or switch off a lamp.

When possible, position a bed under windows to let summer breezes enter without blowing directly on sleepers.

A canopy bed helps to fill the vertical space in a room with high ceilings.

An antique cupboard provides plenty of bedside storage for books, magazines, and other nighttime necessities. And the high top drawer keeps medications and other hazards out of the reach of children.

There is
no need
to be consistently
traditional or
contemporary
when decorating.

Above Cheap tables can be brought back to life with a table skirt. Layer fabric to bring in color and pattern, or use a simple covering to keep the table more subdued.

Right Without much tabletop space on this nightstand, the chair comes in handy as a place to stow a book when it's time to go to sleep.

Right You don't need a dedicated changing table for your baby's nursery—just a dresser with a changing pad placed on top.

Below A bookshelf and comfy chair is all it takes to create a reading nook in any room.

Stock kitchen cabinets and countertops create a wonderful built-in desk in a child's room.

Opposite Storage isessential in a kid's room, especially if two or more siblings share the space.

Left A desk does double-duty as night-stand and large writing surface when bedroom space is tight.

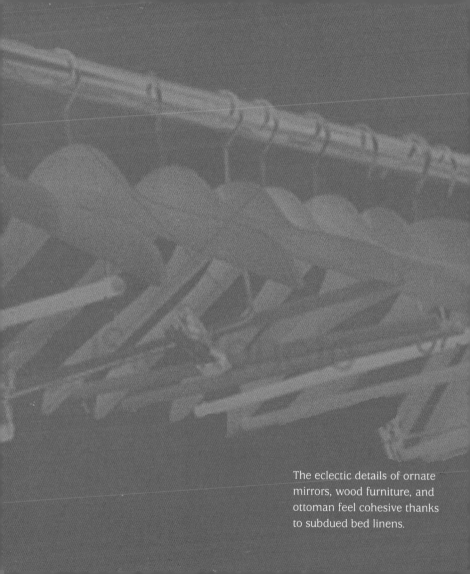

The eclectic details of ornate mirrors, wood furniture, and ottoman feel cohesive thanks to subdued bed linens.

Left A headboard needn't be attached to a bed frame. Just wedge it between the mattress set and the wall.

Right Make your own headboard with ply-wood, cotton batting, and a hand-sewn slipcover.

Bunk beds are the most practical way to sleep
siblings who are share a bedroom. Just make sure
the residents get equal amounts of cubby, drawer,
closet, and display space.

The theme is set with a race car bed complemented by a highway carpet and model of an old-fashioned gasoline pump.

Reupholstered in a fanciful printed fabric that matches the window treatments and wallpaper border, a full-sized chair becomes a cozy child-friendly spot for feedings and readings.

This room is a study in contrasting patterns—from the checkerboard bedspread to the large circular mirror to the vertical lines of the paneling and chair pillow.

decorating
sleeping
spaces

It's amazing how comfortable summertime sleeping becomes when you install a ceiling fan directly over the bed.

Open double-hung windows from the top

to draw out hot air near the ceiling.

Dark walls and
vibrant roller shades
require subtle accesso-
ries. The prints on the
wall complement the
color scheme but take
a backseat.

Create a
child's art
gallery
by hanging
her work in
store-bought
frames.

Displaying your child's artwork in a prominent spot in his room might promote his artistic ambitions

A tabletop of collectibles and framed photos make this comfy space a place for reflection and relaxation.

The white trim helps
to make this room feel
cozier than it is. Simple
décor keeps it clean
and warm.

Above Store-bought shelves are an easy way to add storage and display space to any room.

Left Neutral paint, wallpaper, and furnishings will help a nursery grow with the child.

White gooseneck light fixtures blend well with contemporary architecture and focus bright reading light where needed.

Don't let your bedmate's
Wear a blindfold so the

These hanging lamps need no in-wall wiring; decorative rods hide their plug-in cords.

reading light keep you awake.

glare won't bother you.

Create soft bedroom
light with an accent
lamp, such as the wall
sconce in this nursery
(left) or the small table
lamp in the master
bedroom (below).

A bedside lamp should be high enough to distribute light for reading but not so tall that the bulb is blinding when you're in bed.

The official purpose of this cushioned stool is as a step up to a high bed, but it also provides a spot to stash clothing and books and for sitting on when putting on shoes.

Right The ruffled edges and tiebacks of Priscilla curtains present a dainty look that pairs well with simple, understated furnishings.

Oppostite Sheer curtains offer basic daytime privacy, while the Roman shades underneath offer full coverage at night.

Personalize your window treatments with craft store stencils or a ribbon border and tie-tops.

Above The bold floral print used for these balloon shades, upholstered headboard, and pillow shams energizes an otherwise neutral scheme.

Right Natural light streams through this open headboard, unless the room-darkening curtains are closed for an afternoon nap.

A Japanese shoji screen makes an eye-catching alternative to drapes and can be retrofitted to most existing walls.

....

Give your
bedroom
a different look
for each season
by changing
the bedspread
and shams
with the weather.

....

Bold valances and side panels frame the windows but leave the work of covering and uncovering the openings to fun Roman shades.

A short, squat window is visually enlarged by a shade installed high above it. The neighboring drapery panels installed at a matching height carry out the illusion.

Left Wallpaper cutouts
transform a simple box
cornice into a whimsical
celestial creation.

Opposite A few feet of
PVC pipe in the bottom
hem of a fabric shade
makes it roll up neatly
and exposes the con-
trasting lining.

Oversized knobs are easy for
they transform a basic dresser
Best of all, they're easy to

youngsters to grasp, and
into something colorful and fun.
change as the child grows.

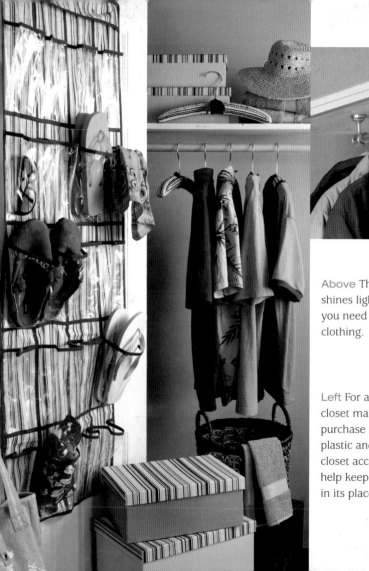

Above This closet rod shines light right where you need it: on your clothing.

Left For a budget closet makeover, purchase ready-made plastic and cardboard closet accessories to help keep everything in its place.

Get rid of clutter
by donating to charity
any everyday item of
clothing that you
haven't worn in
at least a year.

Summer Hats

Summer Shoes

Shorts + Tees

MONDAY

TUESDAY

WEDNESDAY

THURSDAY

FRIDAY

Install bedroom closet shelves and
poles that kids can reach, and they
might—might!—put their own
clothes away.

Right The pull-out trash bin accessories sold for kitchens also make great hampers for bedrooms with built-in cabinets.

Opposite Modular closet kits, which are sold at home stores, include a combination of wood or metal cubbies, racks, shelves, and hangers that are cut to size in the store and that you install yourself.

bathroom
design
& style

"Pillowed" tiles have deep bevels around their edges, making a fully tiled shower enclosure feel like it's inside a fieldstone castle.

Showy wood species, such as bird's-eye maple, are much more affordable when they're just thin veneers applied to a plywood, fiberboard, or resin backing.

A narrow, compact bathroom calls for light colors and simple décor to make it feel spacious and inviting.

Get the look
of stone
for a fraction
of the cost
with faux-stone
porcelain tiles.

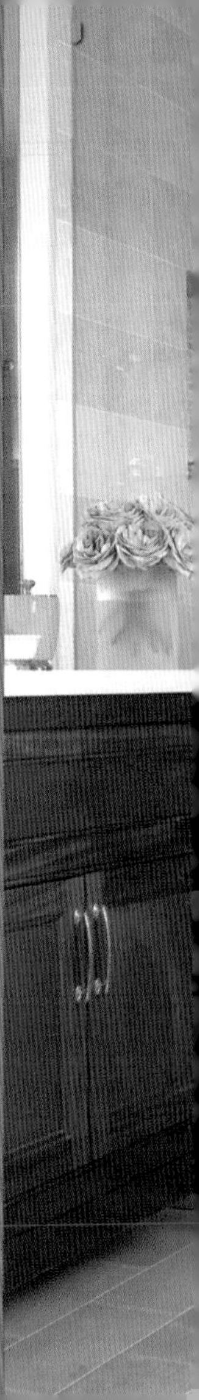

Tiny green onyx tiles are expensive, but when combined with simpler flooring tiles, only a few are needed.

Above Wood wainscot is an inexpensive and eye-catching bathroom upgrade.

Right A tall beadboard wainscot and mantel-like shelf above the soaking tub give this new bathroom a traditional feel.

Installing 4-ft.-high
wainscot is easy.
Purchase 4-ft. by 8-ft.
beadboard sheets,
which need minimal cutting,
and adhere them
with construction adhesive.

Above Contemporary mini-mosaic glass tiles and traditional subway tiles, which mimic the ones used in historic subway stations, look great together.

Right Small tiles are an excellent choice for bathroom floors because the grout lines create traction for wet feet.

Separating the tub from the bathroom's work zones makes for a more
tranquil atmosphere for relaxing soaks.

Refurbished tubs and sinks can be purchased at architectural salvage yards, providing traditional quality at an affordable price.

An old claw-foot tub feels new again thanks to a decorative paint job inspired by the ripples of the ocean's surface.

Hand-cut glass mosaic tiles create a rough, uneven texture that offers a striking contrast to smooth marble floors.

Above Small tiles can easily follow curved profiles, such as this tub wraparound.

Right Translucent glass tiles come in a rainbow of colors, many taking their hues from the recycled bottles used to make them.

Mosaic tiles can be purchased prearranged on mesh backing, which makes installation simple.

Two slightly different patterns create visual interest when the same tiles are used for both floors and walls.

Order at least
10 percent
extra tiles
so you'll have
matching replacements
in case any
ever crack
or chip.

Glass walls help to make both the shower stall and the entire bathroom feel spacious and bright.

A well-placed
shower head and
floor drain

in a tiled shower can create an

open-air version.

Repeating a simple design element—such as a keyhole arch (in the photos here) or wood lattice pattern (opposite)—helps to unify a bathroom.

Adding a washing machine and dryer to an upstairs bathroom makes laundry chores more efficient.

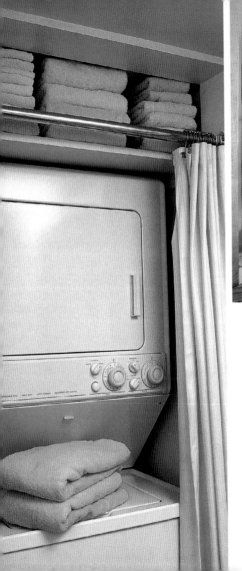

Above White tiles create a clean, sanitary-looking bathroom, while a shift in the size for the walk-in shower adds appealing pattern contrast.

Above Two essentials of child bathtub safety are a pressure-balanced water supply to prevent scalding and nonskid decals to protect against falls.

Left A small stool with nonskid feet brings junior up to the bathroom sink, and a tilting mirror lets him see his own face.

The glossy glaze on these handmade Mexican tiles catches the light and calls attention to their pleasingly irregular shapes.

The fluctuating sizes, shapes, and colors of hand-made tiles lend an appealing irregularity to a wall or floor— and cost many times the price of uniform machine-made tiles.

For a powder room
that needs no medicine
cabinet, a large framed
mirror hangs from
a picture hook above
the sink.

Right Mirrors on opposing walls make a bathroom feel larger—and maximize the lighting, too.

Opposite Hanging a roller shade at the midpoint of a wall of windows provides both privacy and natural light for anyone who wants to soak in this jet tub.

Above A tropically themed tile mosaic brings a playful Caribbean flavor to this bathroom backsplash.

Right Using pricy tiles as accents within a wall of basic tiles is an affordable way to jazz up a tile project.

Swapping out vanity knobs and pulls is a simple and affordable way to refresh the look of a bathroom.

Right A leopard print shade and shower curtain bring an exotic feel to an otherwise subdued bathroom.

Opposite Striped panels located on either side of casement windows have a widening effect.

bathroom
fixtures

A two-legged vitreous
china console sink brings
19th-century elegance to
a new bathroom.

Vessel-style sinks sit on top of the countertop, creating a contemporary look that feels rooted in tradition—and making the most of the space inside a vanity (though vanities aren't required).

Dual sinks make mornings go more smoothly if two people—either adults or children—share a bathroom.

Faucet styles run the gamut from antique re-productions to whimsical new looks. Upgrading a faucet is an easy under-taking for a DIYer.

There are a host of interesting new countertop materials, from poured concrete (left) to engineered stone (bottom) to laminates (right) with color all the way through them, so you won't see the brown or black line common along most laminates' edges.

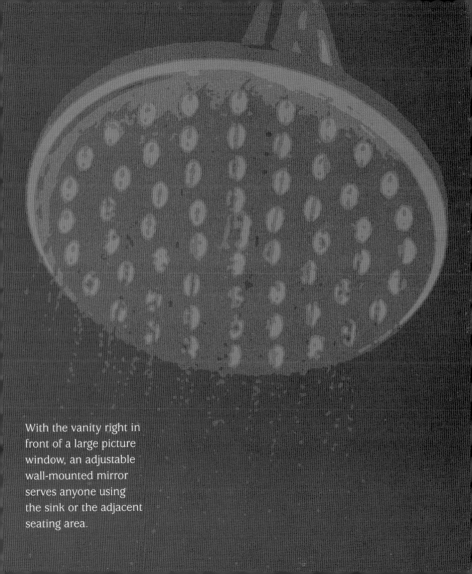

With the vanity right in front of a large picture window, an adjustable wall-mounted mirror serves anyone using the sink or the adjacent seating area.

Independent walk-in showers and soaking tubs offer a more spacious and relaxing bathroom environment than combination shower and tub units.

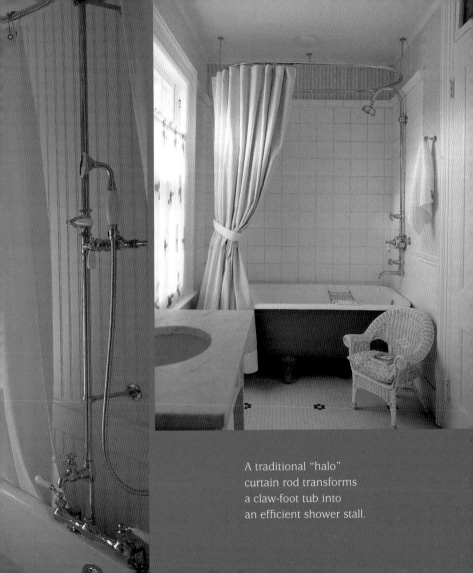

A traditional "halo" curtain rod transforms a claw-foot tub into an efficient shower stall.

Above This modern whirlpool tub has a shape—and fittings—reminiscent of Victorian era bathroom design.

Left Even a standard 5-ft. alcove tub can provide a good soak if it's 12 in. to 16 in. deep (at the overflow valve).

Shower controls belong near the handle side of shower doors so you can turn on the water before climbing in.

For adults,
a body spray jet
makes showering
more luxurious.
For youngsters, it provides
a shower head
at just the right height.

Track-mounted shower heads easily adjust to the size
of the user, so they're ideal for family bathrooms—
or for two adults of very different heights.

Many of today's shower heads offer pressure-assisted
hydro-massage, but this ceiling-mounted sunflower
head provides a decidedly low-tech rain.

Make any shower more sumptuous

by installing an adjustable massaging head.

Copper piping is usually hidden inside the walls, but for this unusual tile tub, it offers a decorative element—and a great spot to hang a washcloth.

A retractable curtain rod maximizes space in a compact bathroom by telescoping out of the way when the shower is not in use.

Pedestal sinks come in many shapes and sizes but need accompanying storage units for traditional bathrooms.

bathroom storage

For any bathroom that kids will use, make sure to select only sturdy furniture and to keep adult supplies on shelves they can't reach.

Store-bought glass or wood shelves are an easy way to add useful surfaces to a bathroom that lacks counter space.

It's easier for guests
to find clean towels
and washcloths
if they're stored on
open shelves
rather than behind
closed doors.

Right A sturdy framed mirror conceals a large built-in medicine cabinet thanks to European-style cabinet hinges, which are hidden entirely behind the mirror.

Opposite Freestanding medicine cabinets offer great storage without taking up much space. And they also add striking design elements.

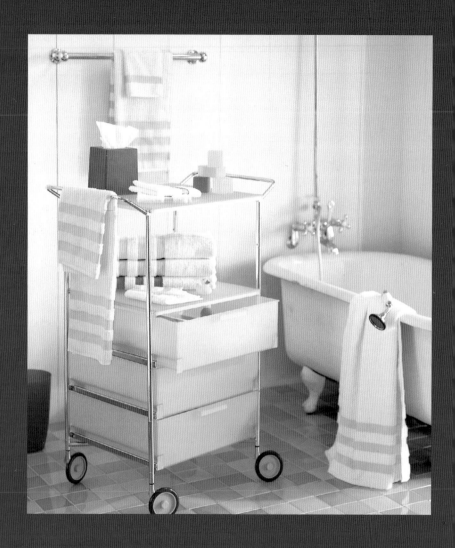

Left Recycle furniture from other rooms to use for bathroom storage; consider a small bedroom dresser or a rolling TV stand, like the one used here.

Opposite Inexpensive home center furniture, such as this colorful utility cart, can add much needed storage to any bathroom.

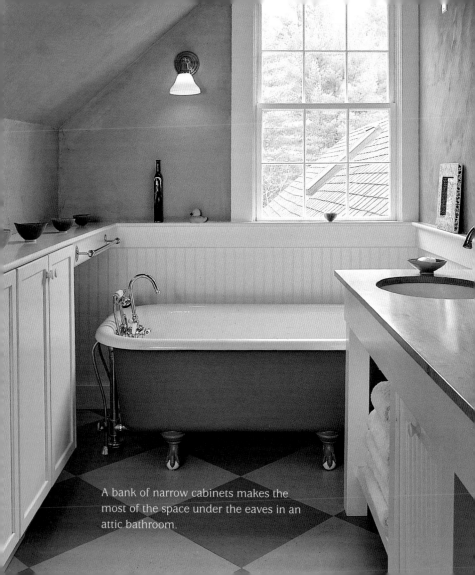

A bank of narrow cabinets makes the most of the space under the eaves in an attic bathroom.

Add bins
and baskets
to the top of cabinets
to hold toiletries
or extra towels.

Whether you use
ordinary hooks or
a custom towel depot
giving each family
member their own spot
for hanging their towel
makes it easy to know
whose is whose.

Keep track of towels by giving each family member a color of their own.

Built-in shelves and cabinets offer the most space-efficient bathroom storage because they can be shallower than either full-sized closets or freestanding cabinets.

Above Use baskets of different sizes and styles to hold anything from reading material to towels to extra toilet paper.

Left A wire shelf provides storage for bathing essentials when there's little or no deck space around the tub.

Right For a bathroom with a shortage of wall space for towel bars, an ingenious carpenter simply widened the window sill and cut a slot in it.

Opposite A wall-mounted coat rack is perfect in a bathroom to hold robes, wet towels, or fresh linens.

Make room for more towels in hooks and bars anywhere

your bathroom by installing
you can find extra space.

A few coats of semi-gloss white paint turn an inexpensive unfinished pine cabinet into a couldn't-live-without-it linen closet.

Mount a shelf over
the sink to provide
easy-access storage.
Glass is the most
unobtrusive material.

Most bathroom storage
accessories come in
ensembles, so that the
style and finish of all
pieces relate.

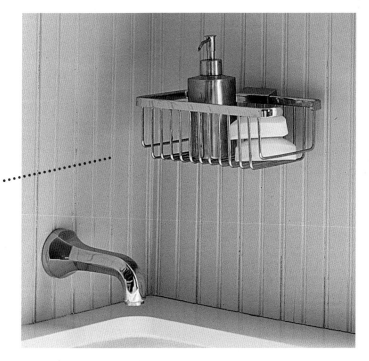

sources

organizations

American Institute
of Architects (AIA)
1735 New York Ave. NW
Washington, DC 200006
www.aiaaccess.com

American Society of
Interior Designers (ASID)
608 Massachusetts Ave. NE
Washington, DC 20002
www.interiors.org

National Association of
Home Builders (NAHB)
1201 Fifteenth St. NW
Washington, DC 20005
www.nahb.org

National Association of
Professional Organizers
www.napo.net

National Association of the
Remodeling Industry (NARI)
4900 Seminary Road #3210
Alexandria, VA 22311
www.nari.org

National Kitchen & Bath
Association
687 Willow Grove St.
Hackettstown, NJ 07840
www.nkba.com

web sites

Decorating Den Interiors
www.decoratingden.com

Dr. Toy
www.drtoy.com

Energy Star
www.energystar.com/gov

Get Decorating
www.GetDecorating.com

HomePortfolio
www.homeportfolio.com

The Building and Home
Improvement Directory
www.build.com

U.S. Consumer Product
Safety Commission
www.cpsc.gov

product sources

Alkco® Lighting
www.alkco.com

American Standard®
www.americanstandard.com

Babybox.com
www.babybox.com

Bed, Bath & Beyond®
www.bedbathandbeyond.com

Bernhardt Furniture
Company
www.bernhardt.com

Blanco®
www.blancoamerica.com

Broadway Panhandler
www.broadwaypanhandler.com

Broyhill Furniture
Industries, Inc.
www.broyhillfurn.com

California Closets®
www.californiaclosets.com

Casabella®
www.casabella.com

CD Storehouse
(800) 829-4203

Chicago Faucets®
www.chicagofaucets.com

Closet Factory
www.closetfactory.com

ClosetMaid®
www.closetmaid.com

The Conran Shop
www.conran.com

The Container Store
www.containerstore.com

Corian®
www.corian.com

Crate & Barrel
www.crateandbarrel.com

Country Floors®
www.countryfloors.com

Dacor®
www.dacor.com

Design Within Reach
www.dwr.com

Elkay®
www.elkayusa.com

Exposures®
www.exposuresonline.com

Filofax®
www.filofax.com

Franke® Sinks & Faucets
www.frankeksd.com

Freedom Bag®
www.freedombag.com

Frigidaire®
www.frigidaire.com

Frontgate®
www.frontgate.com

General Electric®
www.geappliances.com

Graber Window Fashions
www.springs.com

Gracious Home
www.gracioushome.com

Harden Furniture, Inc.
www.harden.com

Halo® Lighting
www.cooperlighting.com

Hold Everything®
www.holdeverything.com

HomeDecInASec
www.homedecinasec.com

Ikea®
www.ikea.com

Jenn-Air®
www.jennair.com

KitchenAid®
www.kitchenaid.com

Kmart™
www.kmart.com

Knape & Vogt
www.knapeandvogt.com

Kohler® Plumbing
www.us.kohler.com

Kraftmaid®
www.kraftmaid.com

The Land of Nod
www.thelandofnod.com

Lamps Plus
www.lampsplus.com

Lane Home Furnishings
www.lanefurniture.com

Levenger®
www.levenger.com

Lightolier®
www.lightolier.com

Mannington, Inc.
www.mannington.com

Maytag®
www.maytag.com

Moen®
www.moen.com

Netkidswear.com
www.netkidswear.com

Poliform
www.poliformusa.com

Posh Tots
www.poshtots.com

Rejuvenation lighting
and hardware
www.rejuvenation.com

Restoration Hardware℠
www.restorationhardware.com

Rev-A-Shelf®
www.rev-a-shelf.com

Rubbermaid®
www.rubbermaid.com

Seabrook Wallcoverings
www.seabrookwallcoverings.com

Serena & Lily
www.serenaandlily.com

Stacks and Stacks
www.stacksandstacks.com

Target®
www.target.com

Thermador®
www.thermador.com

Thomasville Furniture
Industries
www.thomasville.com

Tupperware®
www.tupperware.com

Umbra℠
www.umbra.com

Velux America, Inc.
www.veluxusa.com

Vermont Soapstone
Company
www.vermontsoapstone.com

Viking®
www.vikingrange.com

WallCandy Arts
www.wallcandyarts.com

Wallies
www.wallies.com

The Warm Biscuit Bedding
Company
www.warmbiscuit.com

Wicanders® Cork Flooring
www.wicanders.com

Wolf®
www.subzero.com/wolf

York Wallcoverings
www.yorkwall.com

photo
credits

CHAPTER 1

CHAPTER 2

p. 54–56: Photo: © www.davidduncan-livingston.com.

p. 57: Photo: © Jessie Walker, Design: Adele Lampert Interiors.

p. 58: (top) Photo: © Lisa Romerein; (bottom) Photo: © Wendell T. Webber.

p. 59: Photo: www.davidduncanliv-ingston.com.

p. 60: Photo: © Brian Vanden Brink, Design: Drysdale Associates Interior Design.

p. 61: Photo: © Mark Samu, www.samustudios.com, Design: Lucianna Samu.

p. 63: Photo: © Tim Street-Porter.

p. 64: Kari Haavisto, Design: Brian J. McCarthy.

p. 65: Photo: © Tria Giovan, Design: Phillip Sides.

p. 66: Photo: © Brian Vanden Brink, Design: Polhemus Savory DeSilva Architects.

p. 67: Photo: © Mark Samu, www.samustudios.com, Design: Lucianna Samu.

p. 68–69: Photo© Mark Lohman.

pp. 70–71: Photo: © Wendell T. Webber.

CHAPTER 3

p. 73: Photo: © Mark Samu, www.samustudios.com.

p. 74: Photo: © Rob Karosis.

pp. 76–77: Photo: © Jessie Walker.

pp. 78–79: (top) Photo © Phillip Ennis, Design: Ferfusen, Shamamian & Ratner.

p. 80–81: Photo: © Eric Roth.

p. 83: Photo: © Rob Karosis.

p. 84: Photo: © Olson Photographis, LLC, Design: Ramona Designs.

p. 86: Photo: © Brian Vanden Brink, Design: Jack Silverio.

p. 87: Photo: © Jessie Walker.

p. 88: (top) Photo: © Tim Street-Porter, Design: Tom Callaway; (bottom) Photo: Tim Street-Porter, Design: Hilde Leiaghat.

p. 89: Photo: © Brian Vanden Brink, Design: Green Company Architects.

p. 90: Photo: © www.davidduncanliv-ingston.com.

p. 92: Photo: © Brian Vanden Brink.

p. 93: Photo: © Steve Vierra, www.stevevierraphotography.com.

p. 94: Photo: © Mark Samu, www.samustudios.com.

p. 95: (top) Photo: © Brian Vanden Brink, Design: Drysdale Associates; (bottom) Photo: © www.davidduncan-livingston.com.

p. 96: Photo: © 2006 Carolyn L. Bates, www.carolynlbates.com.

p. 97: Photo: © Jessie Walker.

p. 98: Photo: © Melabee M. Miller.

p. 100: Photo: © Roger Turk/Northlight Photography.

p. 101: Photo: © Mark Lohman.

p. 102: Photo: © 2006 Carolyn L. Bates, www.carolynlbates.com.

p. 103: Photo: courtesy Wallies.

p. 104: Photo: © Lisa Romerein.

p. 105: Photo: © Wendell T. Webber.

p. 106: (left) Photo: © Eric Roth; (right) Photo: courtesy Outwear, LLC.

p. 108: Photo: © Wendell T. Webber.

p. 109: Photo: © www.davidduncanliv-ingston.com.

p. 110: Photo: courtesy California Closet Co.

p. 111: Photo: © Wendell T. Webber.

CHAPTER 4

p. 113: Photo: © Mark Samu, www.samustudios.com.

p. 114: Photo: courtesy Formica Corporation.

p. 115: Photo: Charles Miller, © The Taunton Press, Inc., Design: David Edrington.

p. 117: Photo: © Ellen Silverman.

p. 118: (left) Photo: © Steven Randazzo; (right) Photo: © Eric Roth, Design: Susan Sargent.

p. 120: Photo: courtesy Oceanside Glasstile.

p. 121: Photo: © Brian Vanden Brink, Design: Weston Hewitson Architects, LLC.

p. 122: Charles Miller, © The Taunton Press, Inc., Design: Steve Vanze.

p. 123: Photo: © Tim Street-Porter.

p. 124: Photo: © 2006 Carolyn L. Bates, www.carolynlbates.com.

p. 125: Charles Miller, © The Taunton Press, Inc., Design: Shery Murray-Hanson/Renovation Innovations.

pp. 126–127: Photo: © Mark Samu, www.samustudios.com, Design: Maziar Behrooz/MB Architecture.

p. 128: Photo: © Mark Samu, www.samustudios.com.

p. 129: Scott Phillips, © The Taunton Press, Inc.

pp. 130–131: Photo: © www.davidduncanlivingston.com.

p. 132: Photo: © Steven Randazzo.

p. 134: Photos: © Tim Street-Porter, Design: Suzanne Rheinstein.

p. 135: Photo: © Lance Davies.

p. 137: (left) Photo: Susan Kahn, Design: Liz and Rick O'Leary; (right) Photo: Charles Bickford, © The Taunton Press, Inc.

pp. 138–139: Photos: © Wendell T. Webber.

p. 140: Photo: © Ken Gutmaker.

p. 143: Photo: courtesy Sylvania.

p. 144: Photo: © John Hall.

p. 145: Photo: © Steven Randazzo.

p. 146: Photo: © Peter Mailinowski/Insite.

p. 147: Photo: © 2006 Carolyn L. Bates, www.carolynlbates.com.

p. 148: Photo: © www.davidduncanlivingston.com, Design: McDonald & Moore, Ltd.

p. 149: Photos: Scott Phillips, © The Taunton Press, Inc.

p. 150: Photo: © Melabee M. Miller.

p. 151: Photo: © Jessie Walker.

CHAPTER 5

p. 153: Photo: courtesy Waterworks.

p. 154: Photo: © Brian Vanden Brink, Design: Mark Hutker and Associates, Architects, Inc.

p. 155: (top) Photo: © Tim Street-Porter, Design: Carol Beth Cozen/Cozen Architecture; (bottom) Photo: © Evan Sklar.

p. 156: (top) Photo: © Mark Samu, www.samustudios.com, Design: Ellen Roche Architects; (bottom) Photo: Charles Miller, © The Taunton Press, Inc., Design: Kathy and Steven House of House + House.

p. 157: Photo: © Mark Samu, www.samustudios.com, Design: Sherrill Canet Interiors, Inc.

p. 158: Photo: Carl Weese, © The Taunton Press, Inc.

p. 159: (top) Photo: © Brian Vanden Brink, Design: Christina Oliver Interiors; (bottom) Photo: Mark Samu, www.samustudios.com.

p. 160: (top) Photo: © Steven Randazzo, (bottom) Photo: © Larry Falke, Design: Gary White.

pp. 161–162: Photos: © Mark Samu, www.samustudios.com.

p. 164: Photo: © Tim Street-Porter, Design: Carol Beth Cozen/Cozen Architecture.

p. 165: Photo: © www.davidduncanlivingston.com.

p. 166: Photo: © Brian Vanden Brink.

p. 167: Photo: © Mark Samu, www.samustudios.com, Design: Sherrill Canet Interiors, Inc.

p. 168: Photo: Charles Miller, © The Taunton Press, Inc., Design: Steven Vanze.

p. 169: Photo: Roe A. Osborn, © The Taunton Press, Inc., Design: Laura DuCharme Conboy.

p. 170: Photo: Phillip Fredricks, © National Kitchen & Bath Association.

p. 172: Photo: © www.davidduncanlivingston.com.

p. 173: Photo: © Mark Samu, www.samustudios.com.

p. 174: Photo: © Tim Street-Porter.

p. 176: Photo: © Marcia Trenary, Design: Nora Stombock.

pp. 178–179: Photos: © Grey Crawford, Design: Jim Garramone.

p. 189: Photo: © Wendell T. Webber.

pp. 190 & 193 : Photos: © Rob Karosis.

p. 194: Photo: Brian Pontolilo, © The Taunton Press, Inc.

p. 195: Photo: © Brian Vanden Brink, Design: Weston Hewittson Architects, Inc.

p. 196: Photo: © Tim Street-Porter, Design: Carol Beth Cozen/Cozen Architecture.

p. 197: Photo: courtesy Toto, USA.

p. 198: Photo: © Randi Baird.

p. 199: Photo: © Phillip Ennis, Design: Bradley, Klein, Thiergartner.

p. 200: Photo: © Zachary Gaulkin, Design: Stephen Lauziere.

p. 202: Photo: Carl Weese, © The Taunton Press, Inc.

p. 203: Photo: © Wendell T. Webber.

pp. 204–205: Photos: © Steven Randazzo.

CHAPTER 6

p. 181: Photo: © Durston Saylor, Design: Kaehler Moore Architects.

p. 182: Photo: © Wendell T. Webber.

p. 185: Photo: © Jeremey Samuelson.

p. 186: Photo: Charles Miller, © The Taunton Press, Inc., Design: Bentley and Churchill Architects.

p. 187: Photo: © Brian Vanden Brink.

p. 188: Photo: © Jeremey Samuelson.

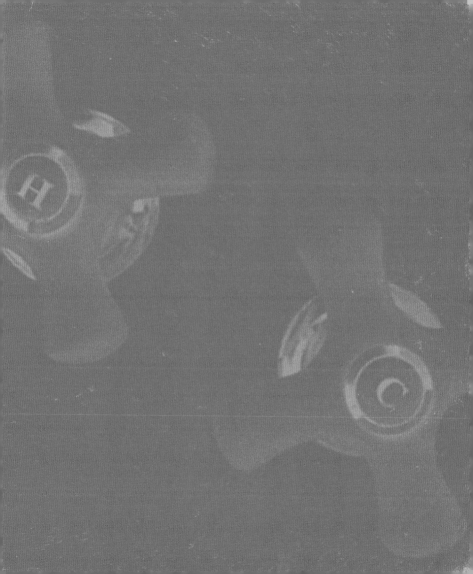